My Pictionary

Scott, Foresman and Company

EDITORIAL OFFICES: Glenview, Illinois

Regional Offices: Sunnyvale, California • Tucker, Georgia •
Glenview, Illinois • Oakland, New Jersey • Dallas, Texas

ISBN: 0-673-12488-6
ISBN: 0-673-28451-4

Copyright © 1990
Scott, Foresman and Company, Glenview, Illinois

Part of this dictionary is also published under the title *Good Morning,
Words!*

112131415-RRW-9998979695 (12488)
  78910-RRW-98979695   (28451)

Introduction: For the Teacher

My Pictionary is designed as a source book of words for children who are just learning to read and write. These young children may have limited experience with written language, but they do have considerable experience with the spoken word. They are capable of learning the relationship between the spoken and written word, and My Pictionary is a colorful invitation to take the first rewarding steps into reading and writing.

The English alphabet has twenty-six letters to represent over forty sounds. It is easy to see why beginning readers often have trouble determining what letter a word starts with. Many words, such as eight and ate, are pronounced alike but are spelled differently. Young children also have great difficulty in finding a word in a long alphabetical list. That is why the words in My Pictionary are arranged in categories familiar to children. These categories group words according to their meaning and function. The words grouped under People, Animals, Places, and Things are nouns; those under What We Do are verbs; and those grouped as Opposites and Helping Words are adjectives and prepositions. Every word in My Pictionary has a picture carefully selected to fully represent that word. Some pictures have labels printed in smaller type to identify additional aspects of the picture, such as feather and wing at **eagle.** In using My Pictionary to find a word, the child need only ask, "What kind of word is it?" Then he or she can find the word, along with others of its kind, under the proper heading. Each category heading is color-coded and has a distinct visual style for easy reference.

The words listed in My Pictionary were chosen from a list prepared especially for this book. The list is made up of words, images, and concepts that children will encounter in kindergarten. Current books and other kindergarten materials—including those that focus on reading, language arts, handwriting, science, health, mathematics, and social studies—were examined and lists were compiled and sorted with the aid of a computer. Most of the 850 words that appear in this book were chosen from this combined list of 1300 words. Also included were words for things commonly found in homes and schools.

An experienced team of editors, designers, illustrators, and teacher consultants have examined every element of My Pictionary to make sure it will stimulate beginning readers to read, to write, to talk, to think, and to learn. A 16-page teacher's guide to using My Pictionary is available to teachers on request.

The Editors

Contents

Contents

Letters of the Alphabet

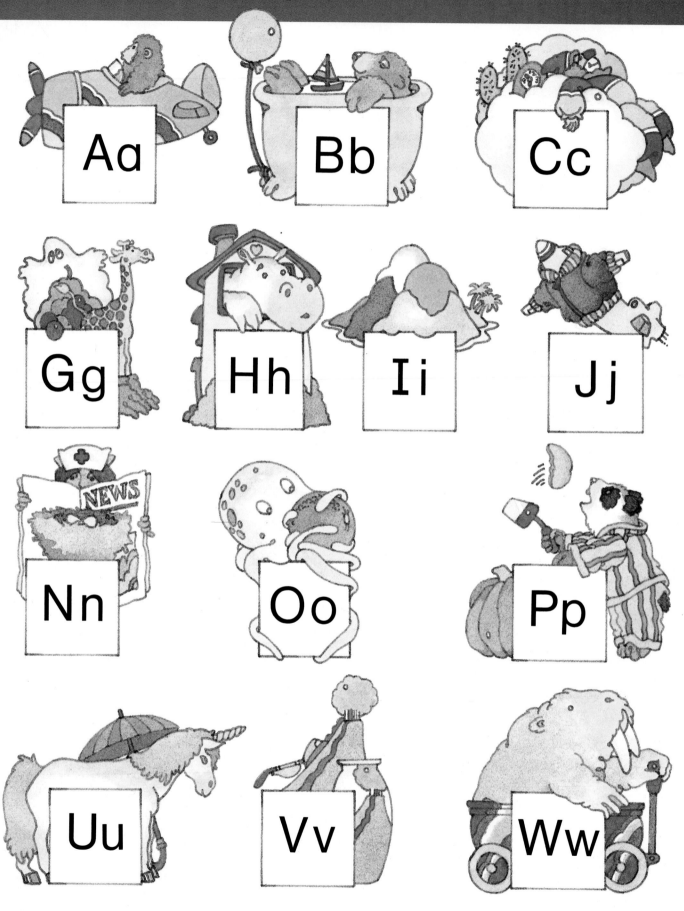

Aa   Bb   Cc

Gg   Hh   Ii   Jj

Nn   Oo   Pp

Uu   Vv   Ww

Dd Ee Ff

Kk Ll Mm

Qq Rr Ss Tt

Xx Yy Zz

People

adults

grown-ups

child

children

woman

women

friends

man

men

baby

babies

twins

People: Family

father
dad
papa
aunt
uncle
cousin
daughter
girl

grandmother

mother

mom

mama

son

boy

grandfather

policewoman

police officers

policeman

salesperson

teacher

doctor

X ray

clown

nurse

astronaut

judge

lawyer

cowboy

baker

carpenter

painter

plumber

electrician

camera

photographer

dentist

librarian

firefighter

mail carrier

soldier

barber

pilot

bus driver

truck driver

secretary

mechanic

chef

farmer

artist

factory worker

People: The Parts of the Body

face

head

stomach

hip

mouth

cheek

back

arm

shoulder

thigh

elbow

hand

heel

ankle

foot

feet

knee

leg

toe

hair

finger

eye

nose

ear

lip

teeth

chin

neck

chest

19

Animals: Pets

dog

puppy

puppies

parakeet

parrot

goldfish

guinea pig

rabbit

bunny

cat

paw

kitten

hamster

gerbil

lamb   sheep

sheep

chickens

turkey

hen

chick

rooster

cow

calf

pig

hog

horse

colt

donkey

goat

23

Animals: Wild Animals

groundhog

raccoon

wolf

beaver

skunk

coyote

chipmunk

fur

squirrel

fox

foxes

Animals: Wild Animals

porcupine

mouse

mice

deer

deer

possum

opossum

bat

polar bear

panda

bear

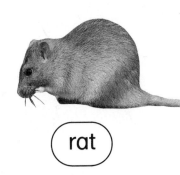

rat

kangaroo

Animals: Wild Animals

turtle

snake

alligator

lizard

iguana

web

spider

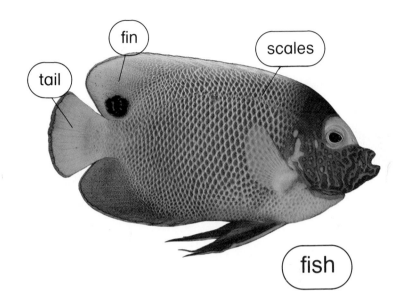

fin

tail

scales

fish

lobster

frog

toad

29

seal

octopus

walrus

whale

dolphin

chimpanzee

ape

gorilla

ape

monkey

monkeys

lion

tiger

leopard

yak

camel

giraffe

zebra

elephant

hippopotamus

rhinoceros

Animals: Birds

goose geese

ostrich

bill

crow

blue jay

34

feather

wing

eagle

robin

owl

hummingbird

cardinal

duck

35

ant

butterfly

caterpillar

fly

beetle

bee

stegosaurus

iguanodon

ankylosaurus

ornitholestes

tyrannosaurus

triceratops

apatosaurus

brachiosaurus

37

Storybook Characters

king

queen

dragon

prince

princess

unicorn

wand

fairy

troll

witch

ghost

giant

monster

elf

Places: Home

attic

bathroom

bedroom

kitchen

dining room

house

basement

roof

garden

doghouse

fence

gate

living room

mailbox

yard

sidewalk

Places: The City

Places: The City

library

school

playground

post office

bakery

shop

store

street

traffic light

farm

barn

silo

pigpen

46

field

tractor

hay

meadow

Places: The Country

mountain

hill

woods

forest

town

bridge

road

country

continent

world

earth

Things: Food

fruit

peach

banana

lemon

plum

grapes

raisins

raspberries

berries

strawberries

orange

cherries

pear

apple

watermelon

tomatoes

tomato

vegetables

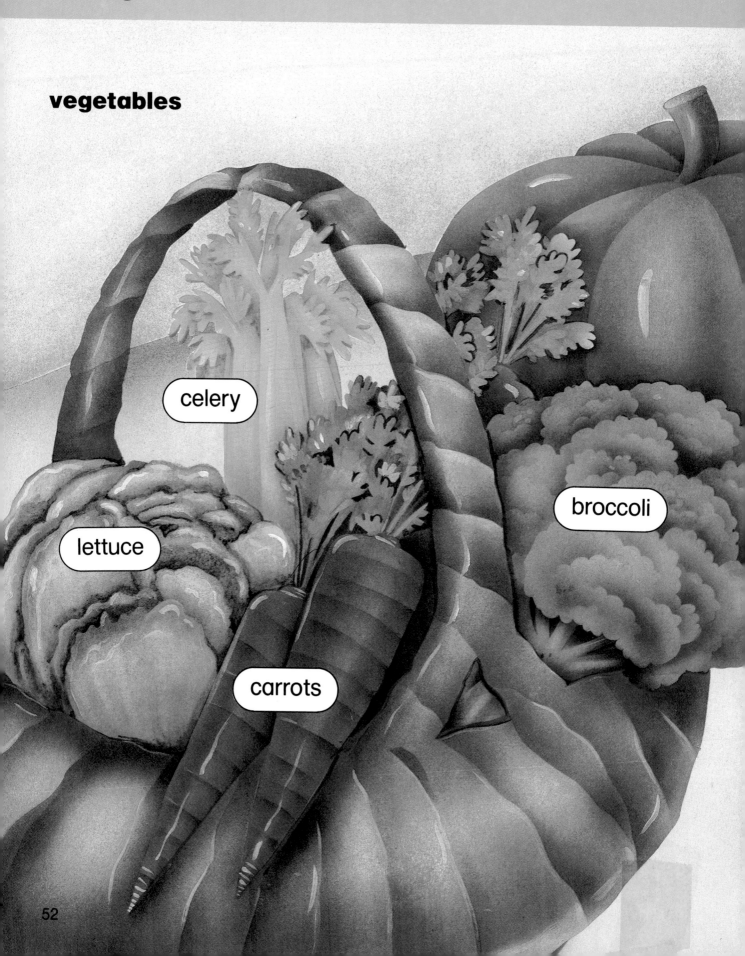

celery

lettuce

broccoli

carrots

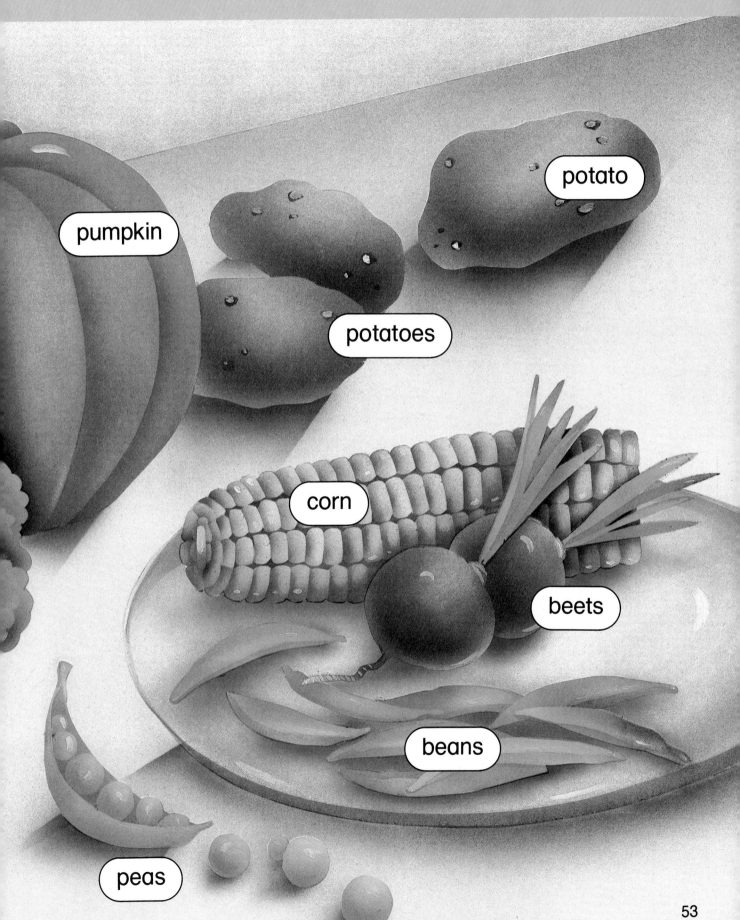

pumpkin

potato

potatoes

corn

beets

beans

peas

popcorn

nuts

salad

peanuts

cake

chicken

cookies

peanut butter

sandwich

cheese

meat

candy

pie

Things: Food

jelly

milk

juice

orange juice

apple juice

eggs

honey

bread

cereal

pancakes

butter

57

hamburger

soup

taco

crackers

fish

pizza

ice cream

Things: Things We Ride In

bike

bicycle

car

automobile

tire

bus

taxi

taxicab

train

jeep

elevator

truck

wagon

wheel

helicopter

van

tractor

boat

jet

plane

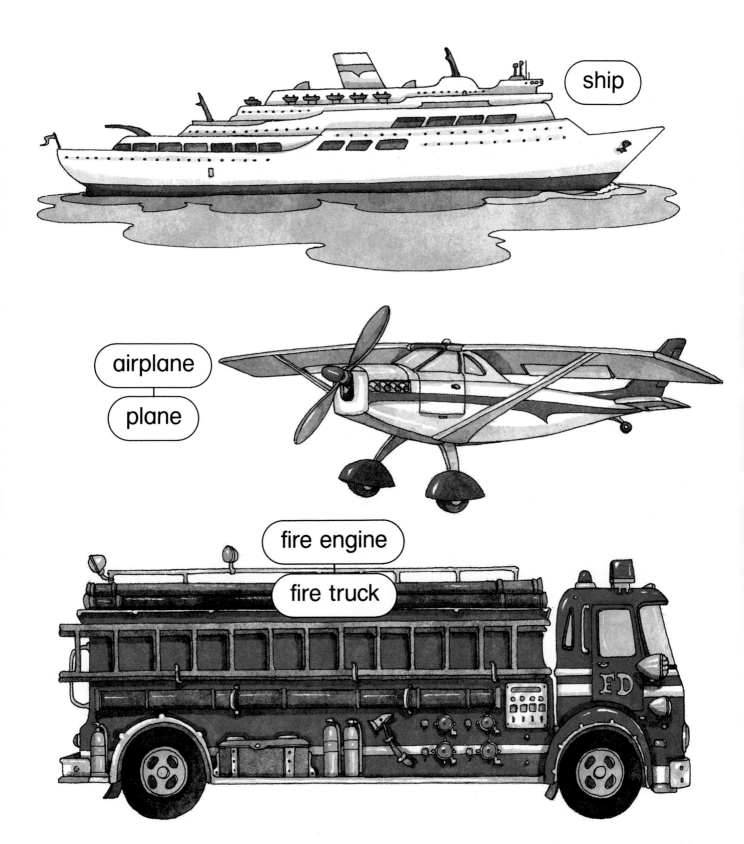

ship

airplane

plane

fire engine

fire truck

bottle

pot

jar

dishes

pan

bowl

glass

cup

napkin

plate

fork

knife

spoon

stairs

steps

key

mail

letter

newspaper

umbrella

picture

lamp

telephone

phone

computer

chair

desk

Things: Things Around the House

candle

clock

wood

basket

radio

fan

towel

soap

washcloth

bathtub

rug

comb

toothbrush

sink

brush

wall

door

bed

floor

pillow

quilt

blanket

curtains

window

crib

straight pin

yarn

safety pin

Things: Things Around the House

ladder
hammer
shovel
broom
mop
vacuum cleaner

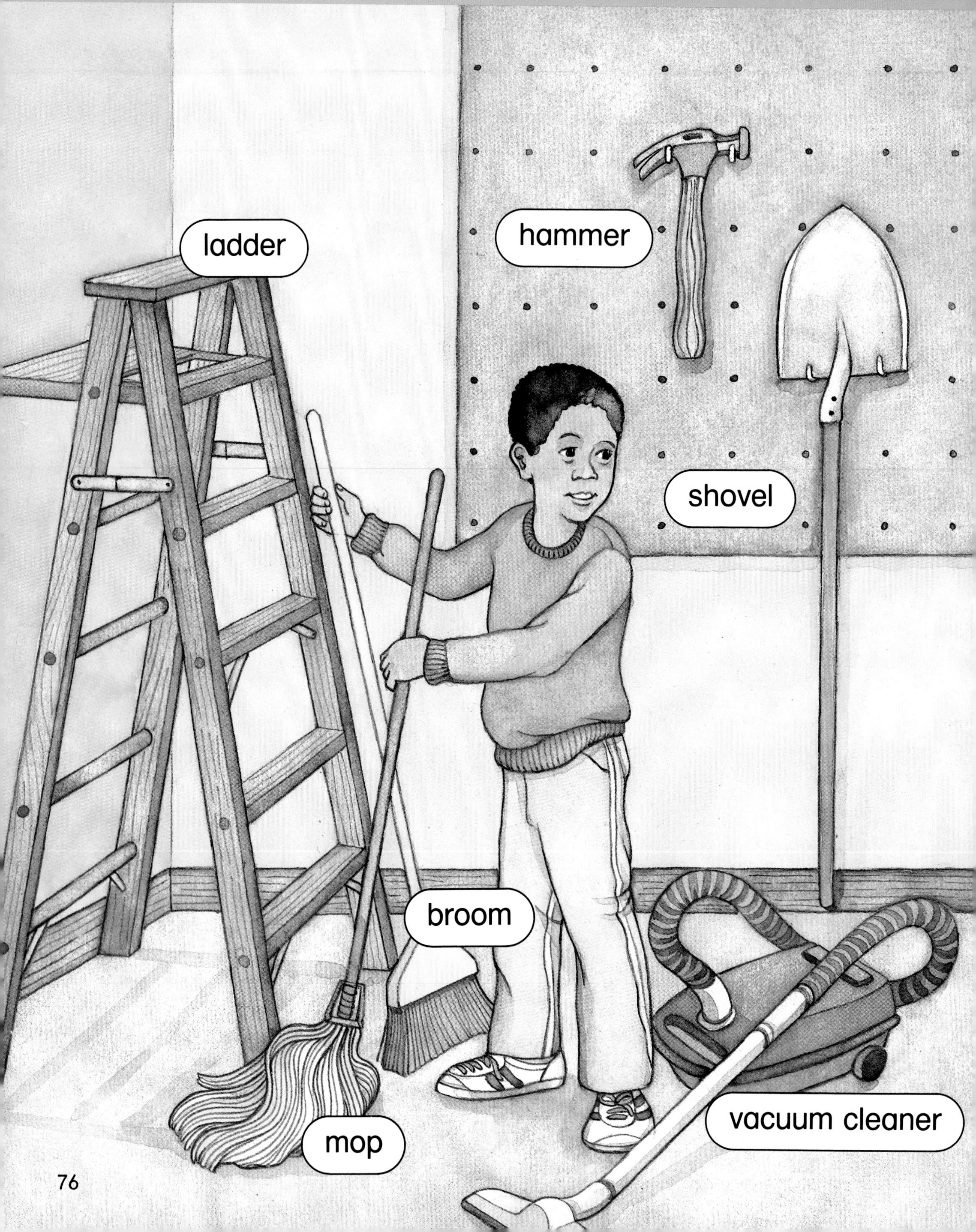

saw

rake

nail

washing machine

washer

dryer

Things: Classroom Things

bulletin board

map

pencil

paste

paper

pen

scissors

crayons

ruler

chalkboard

flag

easel

name

chalk

paint

79

Things: Clothes / Clothing

tie

shirt

necklace

dress

slacks

pants

shoes

vest

sweater

button

pocket

jeans

skirt

Things: Clothes / Clothing

gloves

cap

mittens

coat

zipper

jacket

scarf

hat

raincoat

boots

watch

pajamas

ring

socks

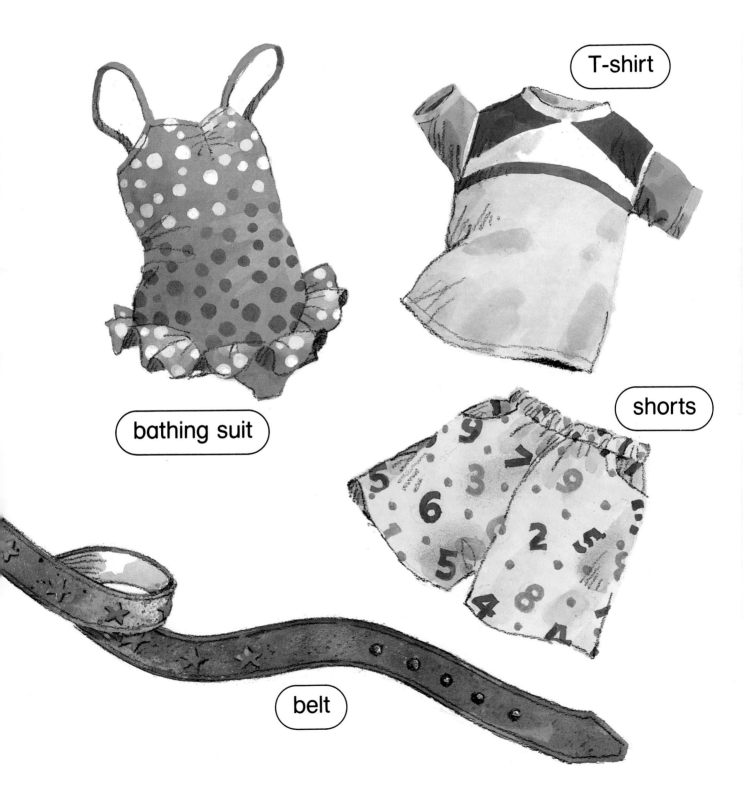

T-shirt

bathing suit

shorts

belt

wind

land

grass

fire

stick

rainbow

volcano

island

water

ocean

sea

seeds

beach

shell

eggshell

nutshell

turtle's shell

seashell

leaf

nest

branch

rain

trunk

tulip

ground

daisy

tree

soil

dirt

bush

flowers

lightning

river

stream

plant

stem

vine

mushroom

root

pond

desert

sun

sand

cactus

cloud

sky

rock

stone

shadow

snow

icicle

ice

snowflake

moon

stars

lake

Things: Playthings

toys

jump rope

marbles

doll

puzzle

piece

kite

whistle

yoyo

puppet

jacks

top

ball

blocks

game

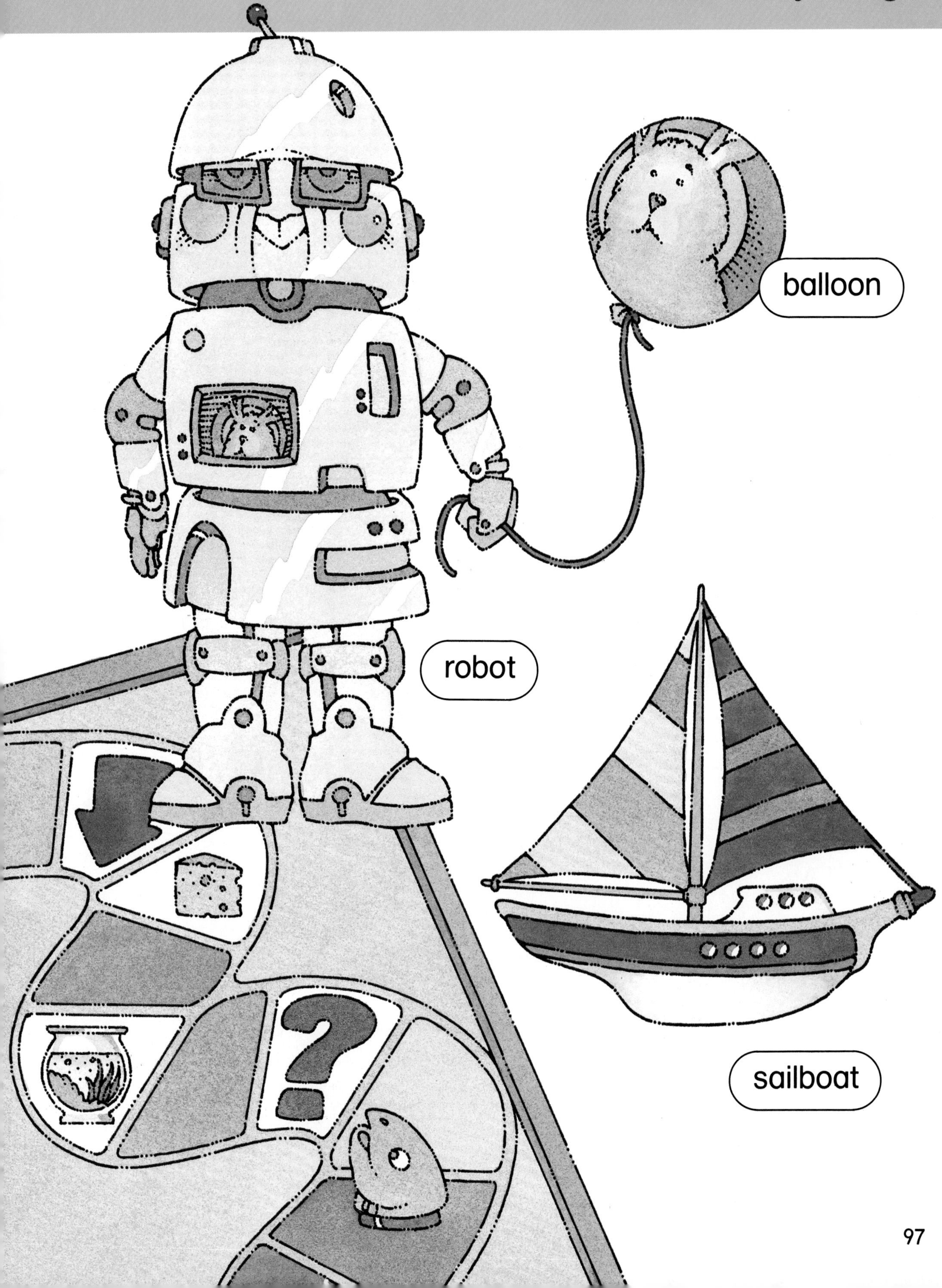

balloon

robot

sailboat

slide

swings

seesaw

sandbox

dump truck

teddy bear

sled

skates

ice skates

roller skates

tricycle

guitar

bells

drum

violin

horn

xylophone

piano

hoop

net

baseball

bat

pitcher

catcher

baseball

helmet

goal post

net

goal

soccer ball

basketball

football

soccer

picnic

birthday

party

present

parade

play

circus

What We Do

sew

read

put

build

write

105

What We Do

dance

hug

dream

hold

carry

sleep

exercise

kick

play

skate

hide

fly

What We Do

wash

brush

comb

grow

dig

plant

108

What We Do

moving van

move

saw

hammer

paint

What We Do

jump

walk

run

fall

throw

climb

hang

follow

swing

skip

hop

catch

bounce

What We Do

sail

fish

swim

count

What We Do

call

show

ride

drive

What We Do

sing

tie

button

zip

draw

cut

fold

color

watch

sit

paste

trace

Opposites

in front of

ahead

in back of

behind

to

from

Opposites

light
day

dark
night

alike
same

different

big
large

little
tiny
small

old

new

120

long

short

dirty

clean

bad

good

go

come

Opposites

before   after

over

under

old

young

short   tall

dry

wet

Opposites

get
take
give

cold
hot

left
right

sad
happy

no
yes

push
pull

123

Opposites

up

down

fast

slow

hard

soft

Helping Words

by

beside

next to

between

across

first

next

last

around

top

at

middle

bottom

into

in

Colors

gray
brown
red
blue
white
pink
yellow
black
orange
green
purple

Shapes

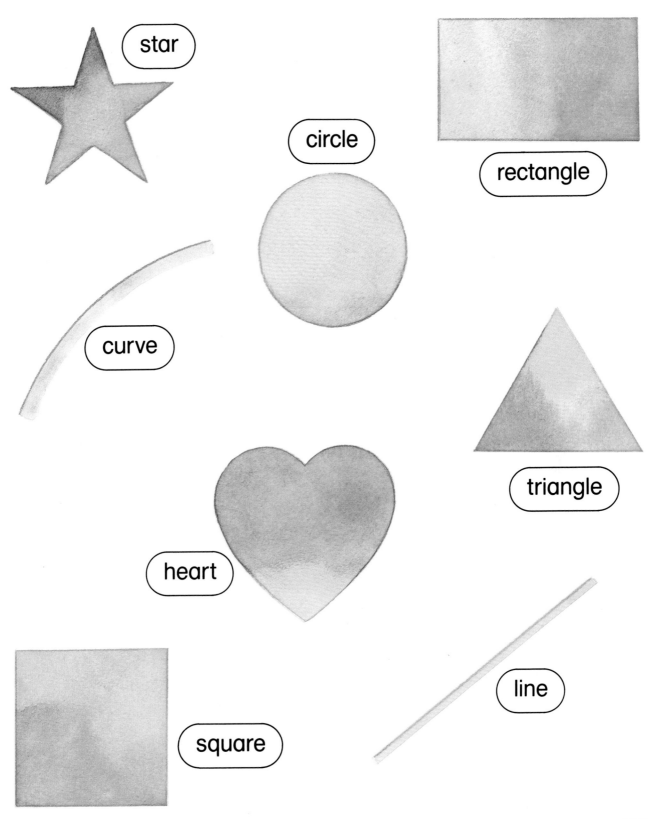

star

circle

rectangle

curve

triangle

heart

square

line

Numbers

0 (zero)

1 (one)

2 (two)

3 (three)

4 (four)

5 (five)

6 (six)

7 (seven)

8 (eight)

9 (nine)

10 (ten)

penny 1¢

pennies

nickel 5¢

dime 10¢

quarter 25¢

one dollar $1.00

five dollars $5.00

Months of the Year and Holidays

January

February

March

valentine

Valentine's Day

April

May

June

Months of the Year and Holidays

July

August

September

Independence Day

Fourth of July

October

November

December

jack-o'-lantern

Hanukkah

Halloween

Thanksgiving

Christmas

Seasons

spring

summer

fall

winter

Days of the Week and Time of Day

Sunday

Monday

Tuesday

Wednesday

Thursday

Friday

Saturday

morning

afternoon

night

Index

Index

Index

Index

Artists

Pages 6–7—Dick Martin
Pages 8–19—Kees de Kiefte
Page 37—Alan Bernard
Pages 38–39—Chi Chung
Pages 40–49—Linda Kelen
Pages 50–59—Patti Boyd
Pages 60–65—Lane Yerkes
Pages 66–67—Blanche Sims
Pages 68–69—Lane Yerkes
Pages 70–73—Blanche Sims
Pages 74–75—Chi Chung
Pages 76–77—Chi Chung/Robert Masheris
Pages 78–79—Blanche Sims
Pages 80–85—Janet LaSalle
Pages 86–93—Lynn Adams
Pages 94–99—Dick Martin
Pages 100–101—Bob Knight
Pages 102–103—Chi Chung
Pages 104–105—Gioia Fiammenghi
Pages 106–107—Brian Karas
Pages 108–109—Robert Alley
Pages 110–111—Brian Karas
Pages 112–113—Robert Alley
Pages 114–115—Brian Karas
Pages 116–117—Gioia Fiammenghi
Pages 118–119—Roberta Collier
Pages 120–123—Carolyn Bracken
Pages 124–125—Roberta Collier
Pages 126–127—Julie Durrel
Pages 128–129—Robert Masheris
Page 130—Georgia Shola
Pages 132–133—Randall Enos
Pages 134–135—Andrea Eberbach

Photographers

Page 20—dog: Robert Carr/Bruce Coleman Inc.
puppy, goldfish: Zig Leszczynski/Animals Animals
puppies: Ginger Chih/Peter Arnold, Inc.
parakeet: Robert Pearcy/Animals Animals
parrot: Hans Reinhard/Bruce Coleman Inc.
Page 21—guinea pig, hamster: Hans Reinhard/Bruce Coleman Inc.
rabbit/bunny: Jane Burton/Bruce Coleman Inc.
cat & kitten: Robert Pearcy/Animals Animals

gerbil: E. R. Degginger/Bruce Coleman Inc.
Page 22—lamb & sheep: Grant Heilman/Grant Heilman Photography
sheep (plural), chickens: Hans Reinhard/Bruce Coleman Inc.
turkey, rooster: Ben Goldstein/Valenti Photography
hen: Richard Kolar/Animals Animals
chick: Robert Pearcy/Animals Animals
Page 23—cow & calf: Charlton Photos
pig/hog, goat: Hans Reinhard/Bruce Coleman Inc.
pony & colt: J. C. Allen & Son, Inc.
donkey: L. L. T. Rhodes/Animals Animals
Page 24—raccoon: Hans Reinhard/Bruce Coleman Inc.
groundhog, beaver: Wayne Lankinen/Bruce Coleman Inc.
wolf: Stephan J. Krasemann/DRK Photo
skunk: Bob & Clara Calhoun/Bruce Coleman Inc.
coyote: Wayne Lynch/DRK Photo
Page 25—chipmunk, squirrel: Zig Leszczynski/Animals Animals
fox: Breck P. Kent/Animals Animals
foxes: Hans Reinhard/Bruce Coleman Inc.
Page 26—porcupine: Kenneth W. Fink/Bruce Coleman Inc.
mouse: Breck P. Kent/Animals Animals
mice: Jane Burton/Bruce Coleman Inc.
deer: Tom Edwards/Animals Animals
deer (plural): Leonard Lee Rue III/Bruce Coleman Inc.
possum/opossum: Martin L. Stouffer/Animals Animals
Page 27—bat: Jane Burton/Bruce Coleman Inc.
polar bear: Johnny Johnson/Animals Animals
panda: J. L. G. Grande/Bruce Coleman Inc.
bear: Charles Palek/Animals Animals
rat: Hans Reinhard/Bruce Coleman Inc.
kangaroo: Patti Murray/Animals Animals
Page 28—turtle: Leonard Lee Rue III/Bruce Coleman Inc.
snake, lizard: Hans Reinhard/Bruce Coleman Inc.
alligator: C. C. Lockwood/DRK Photo
iguana: Alan Blank/Bruce Coleman Inc.
Page 29—spider: Stephen J. Krasemann/DRK Photo

fish: Zig Leszczynski/Animals Animals
lobster: Scott Johnson/Animals Animals
frog: Hans Reinhard/Bruce Coleman Inc.
toad: John Gerlach/DRK Photo
Page 30—seal: Alan G. Nelson/Animals Animals
octopus: Jane Burton/Bruce Coleman Inc.
walrus: Stephen J. Krasemann/DRK Photo
whale: C. Allan Morgan/Peter Arnold, Inc.
dolphin: Mickey Gibson/Animals Animals
Page 31—chimpanzee/ape: J. & D. Bartlett/Bruce Coleman Inc.
gorilla/ape: Hans Reinhard/Bruce Coleman Inc.
monkey: Rod Williams/Bruce Coleman Inc.
monkeys: Zig Leszczynski/Animals Animals
Page 32—lion: Charles Palek/Animals Animals
tiger: Zig Leszczynski/Animals Animals
leopard: Belinda Wright/DRK Photo
yak: Bruce Coleman/Bruce Coleman Inc.
camel: Mickey Gibson/Animals Animals
Page 33—giraffe: Stefan Meyers/Animals Animals
zebra: N. Myers/Bruce Coleman Inc.
elephant: Zig Leszczynski/Animals Animals
hippopotamus: Simon Trevor/Bruce Coleman Inc.
rhinoceros: Jane Burton/Bruce Coleman Inc.
Page 34—goose: Margot Conte/Animals Animals
geese: Henry R. Fox/Animals Animals
ostrich: Zig Leszczynski/Animals Animals
crow: Hans Reinhard/Bruce Coleman Inc.
blue jay: Breck P. Kent/Animals Animals
Page 35—eagle: Johnny Johnson/DRK Photo
owl, robin: E. R. Degginger/Animals Animals
hummingbird: Alan G. Nelson/Animals Animals
cardinal: Zig Leszczynski/Animals Animals
duck: Donald E. Waite/Bruce Coleman Inc.
Page 36—butterfly: Eric Dragesco/Bruce Coleman Inc.
ant: G. I. Bernard/Animals Animals
caterpillar: Breck P. Kent/Animals Animals
fly: Avril Ramage/O. S. F./Animals Animals
beetle: Hans Reinhard/Bruce Coleman Inc.
bee: Donald Specker/Animals Animals
Page 131—Scott, Foresman staff

a b c d e f g h i j
k l m n o p q r s
t u v w x y z
A B C D E F G H
I J K L M N O P
Q R S T U V W
X Y Z , ' . ?
1 2 3 4 5
6 7 8 9 10